AF542000

VICTORY MANTRA

THE LEADER'S PATH TO SUCCESS

PUSHPESH PANT

RUPA

Published by
Rupa Publications India Pvt. Ltd 2014
7/16, Ansari Road, Daryaganj
New Delhi 110002

Sales centres:
Allahabad Bengaluru Chennai
Hyderabad Jaipur Kathmandu
Kolkata Mumbai

ISBN: 978-81-291-3561-2

First impression 2014

10 9 8 7 6 5 4 3 2 1

Printed at Nutech Photolithographers, New Delhi

Contents

Introduction

Not just India, but the entire world has been stunned by the historic victory registered by the Narendra Modi-led Bharatiya Janata Party (BJP) in the 2014 Lok Sabha elections. It would be wrong to say that nobody had anticipated it, but no one could have imagined the scale of the victory. After the results came out, the defeated parties even started blaming supernatural forces for the enormity of their defeat.

Some have tried to point out how this 'miracle' was made possible by millions, even billions spent on advertisements that apparently hoodwinked the innocent and ignorant voters of India. This school of thought insists that it was the partisan effort of paid media—who created a charismatic Superman-like image of Modi—which triggered a 'wave' that eventually became a tsunami, sweeping everybody else aside. One can understand the dejection and disbelief of the discredited losers, who simply cannot accept reality. But it should be clear to any rational person that there was no 'magic' behind the Modi victory. Dig a little deeper and it becomes clear that the foundation of this victory was laid upon some time-tested principles or mantras that almost all successful leaders have employed in the past.

The first step towards success is the ability to be extremely clear about the destination. You could call this single-minded focus on the goal. It is only when you know your destination that you can start searching for the path and take the first step. All big tasks are invariably fraught with hurdles and challenges along the way. You need confidence and courage to face them. A strong sense of self-belief and the ability to keep one's supporters highly motivated is a must to complete a journey successfully. For this, a good leader invokes and employs the mantra of optimism and positive thinking.

Next comes the task of preparing well for the aforesaid journey; call it planning or strategy, if you will. But the fact is that it is crucial to prepare a detailed road map, to anticipate the pitfalls and dangers on the path and to work out in advance how the enemy would try to scupper your way using diversions and traps. To have clarity about your strengths and weaknesses is an integral part of this strategy. The lives of numerous leaders tell us one thing: they all had a clear and focused war management strategy. Successful leaders make full use of their strengths by always being focused on their goal and never wavering from it, no matter what the provocation or problem. This helps them sustain self-confidence and keep their followers motivated.

All the planning and strategizing would be futile if the leader does not consistently display determination, tireless work and self-discipline. No goal can be achieved without these mantras. There have been many leaders in history whose victories have been labelled historic, unprecedented and even miraculous. All of them have candidly admitted, to paraphrase Thomas Edison, that genius has accounted for just 1 per cent of their victory and success while hard work accounts for 99 per cent. The only way leaders can persevere tirelessly, without complaints about the extreme stress involved—both physical and mental—and keep marching towards their goal, is when they rise above narrow self-interests. A successful leader has a vision and a passion to do something positive for fellow human beings and transform their lives. It is this that enables a leader to make personal sacrifices along the way. And this is possible only if you are imbued with the spirit of service, hope and patriotism.

An even bigger challenge is to persuade and convince others to become active and enthusiastic partners in this journey. That is possible when leaders display the uncanny ability to fuse their dreams with the aspirations of the common man. You cannot merely ask your followers to make sacrifices to help you achieve victory. It is important to understand that a leader can inspire and motivate others only if they themselves are convinced about defending or advancing a principle, an ideal or even an ideology. Also, motivation is possible only when a general or a leader is in constant communication with his followers and partners. Positive and continuous communication is the key; leaders who fail to effectively communicate lose trust and find it very difficult to regain it. Effective communication also entails willingness to innovate, take risks and adopt new techniques and technology.

Modi has proved to be a master at communication. His powerful campaign virtually dominated the social media. There can be no doubt that the use of Twitter, Facebook, Google Hangouts and 3D holograms during rallies gave him a decisive edge over his opponents. This enabled him to not just reach out to more voters, but also to convince them that he shares their aspirations for a better future.

The mantras of success and victory employed by Modi have nothing to do with black magic or tantric powers. It was his ability to use certain time-tested and timeless strategies in an effective manner. It was strong self-belief, tireless work, the ability to not be frightened or sidetracked by obstacles during the journey and the visible willingness to inspire followers as partners that brought victory to Modi. Any human being is capable of using these mantras to achieve their individual goals. As Modi has shown, you can really make your own destiny. It is not luck but hard work that wins the day. Always.

1

Clear Vision and Focus on Goal

The first mantra of victory is complete clarity about the goal. This helps the warriors in their preparation and in honing their aim on the battlefield. Once you lose sight of your goal, you could go on endlessly and fruitlessly searching for new destinations.

It is often said that wise people select goals that are reachable and realistic. There is also a famous proverb that goes, 'Cut your coat according to your cloth'. But the interesting thing is that a person who achieves 'unprecedented' and 'historic' victories usually chooses destinations that appear out of reach to ordinary people. The fact is that voyagers would never have discovered new countries and continents if they had chosen to travel the well-trodden path. It is only the brave and ambitious who veer off the known tracks in quest of their goals, who achieve the seemingly impossible. When legendary mountaineer Reinhold Messner declared that he intended to single-handedly conquer all peaks above 8,000 metres in the world, and that too without oxygen, almost everyone dismissed his ambition as an impossible one. But when Messner achieved his goal, the world was compelled to admit that nothing is impossible if a man sets about to achieve it and pursues that goal relentlessly. The very term 'leader' means paving the way for others by setting an example through personal efforts. Only those who are clear about their destination can show the way to others.

Modi never had a doubt about his goal. Soon after the elections were announced and the battle lines drawn, he publicly proclaimed that his war is a war to win a majority. He kept insisting that the BJP was aiming for at least 272 Lok Sabha seats. A lot of people, including (even) some of his supporters, then thought that Modi was indulging in bombastic bravado. A majority were of the opinion, at first, that the BJP would at best manage to win between 180 to 190 seats. The idea was that Modi would somehow manage to attract some allies to get the required majority to form a government.

Like a true leader and general, Modi continually exhorted

his supporters in every public rally and meeting to ensure that 300 lotuses (the BJP's party symbol) bloomed in the elections. The result was that Modi's supporters never had any doubts about what their eventual and bigger goal was. With the final destination clear, Modi and his supporters found it easier to surmount obstacles along the way.

Of course, till he demonstrated that he walked the talk, critics mocked at him for talking about such unattainable goals. The constant refrain was: how could he alone win a majority? Did it mean that all BJP candidates will win, and that too in states like Tamil Nadu and West Bengal where winning even one seat looked like a pipe dream? Mamata Banerjee would never allow Modi to gain a foothold in her state. The Congress appeared formidable in traditional bastions like Maharashtra, Assam and Karnataka. Did anyone even recognize Modi in a state like Odisha? Mission 272+ was nothing but tall talk. But Modi kept marching ahead, ignoring these constant jibes, and never wavered from his goal.

Modi displayed tremendous ability to break down his ultimate goal to a series of smaller, realistic targets and was clever enough to anticipate obstacles and plan for them. One part of the goal was number-crunching, while the other challenge was extending the geographical limits of the BJP. Modi neatly surmounted these by crafting an entirely new electoral strategy to reach his destination. His strategy was simple—to capture the hearts and minds of the youth of the country. Everyone kept talking about how the 2014 elections would see about 10 crore new voters. Leaders of other parties were content with trying to woo these new voters by using the traditional tricks of identity politics. But Modi kept hammering away a simple message to this young, restless and aspirational cohort of voters—to be able to realize our dreams, hopes and aspirations for a better future, we must break out of the old shackles of voting on the basis of caste, religion and language and focus instead on development and development alone. Modi's clarion call of development was not seen by voters as a mere electoral slogan. Soon, he went from being just the leader of a party and just the chief minister of a state to someone who could harness technology to deliver on the promise of development on a national scale. He was seen as someone who had the credibility and competence to create jobs, to revitalize agriculture and industry and to fight a decisive battle against corruption. Before anyone realized it, Modi had emerged as a powerful national leader.

To win the hearts of the youth, Modi started communicating directly with students of famous colleges and institutions such as the IITs. Long before elections were announced or he was made the prime ministerial candidate, he spoke at a business conclave organized by some students of the Shri Ram College of Commerce in

Delhi. Many 'secular and progressive' people opposed this interaction; quite a few students and teachers even boycotted the conclave. But the speech delivered by Modi proved to be a big hit and supporters as well as opponents kept debating and discussing it for days on end. After this success, Modi visited the IITs and many private universities to directly interact with the students. He received enthusiastic welcomes in almost all these places. He knew very well that if he could persuade these youngsters to support him and his vision for India, they in turn would convince their peers.

Another Modi success story is of how he got the support of the Citizens for Accountable Governance (CAG), an organization comprising students, lawyers, engineers, teachers, bankers, managers, journalists and other professionals. Initially apolitical, the CAG decided to openly and strongly support Modi after he interacted with leading members of this group. He had credible answers to their questions about bringing good governance to India.

In his quest for 272+ seats, Modi paid particular attention to states such as Uttar Pradesh, Rajasthan and Bihar, well before the elections were formally announced. If you add Delhi and Haryana to the list, it becomes clear that Modi was targeting the so-called Hindi heartland in a big way. There were two reasons for this. First, a lot of MPs came from these states. And second, these states, for the most part recently, had been ruled by parties that were implacably opposed to the BJP and Modi.

It has been said by many critics that Modi used the politics of division and divisiveness to win the elections. No doubt, there is an element of truth to this. But the interesting thing is that Modi used this old-style political strategy not to 'divide' but to polarize a large segment of voters in his favour. He was clearly successful in imparting credibility to his powerful slogan of '*Sabka saath, sabka vikaas*', and merged this publicly stated aim seamlessly with the eventual goal of 272+ seats.

Hundreds of thousands of unknown and anonymous youngsters joined his mission to get a majority for the BJP and worked ceaselessly at the grass-roots level. Around 100,000 volunteers extensively used information technology and social media to try and send the core message of Modi to every nook and corner of India. Many of them had jobs in countries like England and the United States and had either quit their jobs or taken leave to become proud soldiers in this decisive battle to make Modi the prime minister. The Anna Hazare movement, about one and a half years back, had inspired a similar kind of enthusiasm and passion amongst the youth. It is important to mention this just to understand how common citizens and the youth can be willing to sacrifice personal short-term interests if they are inspired by a credible message and voice of patriotism and national service. This spirit of service and duty enables people to constantly strive for victory even as they encounter many ups and downs along the way.

This indeed was the first mantra of Modi's success: his ability to fuse and merge his goal with the dreams and aspirations of people. Every time he talked about Mission 272+, people realized that it would be futile to expect an accountable and performing government without giving a majority to Modi. No majority for Modi would mean the daily drudgery of corruption and struggle. Thanks to this, ordinary voters started looking at Mission 272+ as their own goal.

2

Courage and Confidence

There is an interesting story from the Mahabharata where Arjuna is striving for excellence in archery. The target is a bird sitting on a tree trunk. So focused is Arjuna that all he can see is the eye of the bird; not the bird's body, nor the tree and nothing else around him. When mentor and teacher Dronacharya asks him about what he sees, he replies, 'The eye'. When the other young archers with him are asked the same question, some describe the tree, others mention the branches, while a few manage to spot the bird against the foliage. Arjuna, as is well known, outdid them all in archery. No surprise then that total, concentrated and unwavering focus on the target or goal is essential to achieve success.

But all the focus and clarity might not yield results if you do not have self-confidence and bravery. Successful leaders not only display courage and confidence themselves, but also have the ability to inspire their followers to be as courageous. Arjuna's unmatched prowess with the bow would have been wasted if he had given in to his misgivings on the battlefield of Kurukshetra.

An old saying puts it so aptly: fortune favours the brave. One of the most legendary generals known for his battlefield brilliance, Napoleon Bonaparte used to keep repeating the word 'courage' when asked about the one key ingredient required for victory. It is only a courageous person who can achieve the difficult or even the impossible. It is only he or she who becomes successful. It is often in your mind that you win or lose the battle.

When we try to understand the secret of Modi's success, it is important to appreciate how he sustained his courage and conviction for more than a year and also succeeded in inspiring his partners and followers to stay consistently motivated and optimistic.

When Modi made his intentions clear to the world, even the announcement of the elections was quite far away. Virtually no one could imagine how Modi could upstage so many formidable BJP leaders to emerge as the party's prime ministerial candidate; the idea of him becoming the unquestioned general leading his party through the electoral battlefield was even more remote. Even Modi's supporters were hesitant to suggest that the BJP under him would win a majority. But Modi had courage and conviction. And he unabashedly borrowed from Barack Obama's historic presidential campaign of 2008. Used to delivering his speeches in Hindi, Modi never hesitated to use the now-legendary Obama slogan during his rallies: 'Yes we can, yes we will.'

His critics mocked him for imitating Obama. But the fact is that there was hidden brilliance in this art of imitation. In 2008, Obama had correctly assessed that Americans were craving for change so he made change the central theme of his campaign. Modi did the same. The citizens of India were fed up with ten years of back-breaking inflation and brazen corruption and were yearning for change. It must be understood here that this desire for change in India was not limited to choosing one party or alliance over the other. Aspirational young Indians were becoming acutely aware that the seeming helplessness of governments at the centre and the states were not just denting the image of India but also threatening their job opportunities and their future.

The concentration of power in just a few hands and families had made a mockery of the concept of democracy. The biggest disappointment for Indians was the prime minister of the previous regime. It was clear that the weak PM was unable to control and manage his own cabinet ministers; and he didn't appear to even make an effort to curb the growing lawlessness in the country. People were becoming increasingly convinced that this paralysed government could deliver neither economic growth nor social justice. The government looked tired and defeated, and there was no hope of any change from this regime. No big leader from the Congress—and there are so many of them—was able to inspire confidence or connect with ordinary Indians. It was against this backdrop that Modi unleashed his 'Yes, we can' slogan. And Indians started thinking that change might just be possible with Modi as the leader.

Modi had already acquired the image of being an aggressive and dynamic leader as the chief minister of Gujarat. His campaign reinforced this image and made him a larger-than-life figure. He made it a point to climb briskly up the stairs of a podium to address public rallies; he mastered the art of keeping crowds mesmerized with his public oratory; and he ended almost every speech with three resounding chants of the emotional battle cry, '*Vande Mataram*', that was repeated enthusiastically by the crowds. After Independence, '*Vande Mataram*' had been accorded a status equal to that of the National Anthem. However, the 'disrespect' shown to the song by some MPs was sadly overlooked and underplayed by the earlier United

Progressive Alliance (UPA) government. This had caused anguish to a large number of Indians. Modi leveraged this 'hurt' to his advantage. Ordinary Indians attending these rallies were compelled to think that there was something refereshingly different about this man.

The crowning moment of his campaign came during the Hunkar Rally in Patna on 27 October 2013. The poise and confidence with which Modi continued his speech despite a series of blasts in the city—some of them at the very venue where he was to address the crowd—showed that this man had courage in abundance. When there was no stampede despite the bomb blasts and Modi continued, cynical commentators watching the action on TV screens found it hard to allege that Modi roars only in his den and doesn't have the courage to challenge others in their strongholds.

In Lucknow, he used biting humour to take on the rulers and enthralled the audience by proclaiming that to make Uttar Pradesh another Gujarat, you need a fifty-six-inch chest. Even as he delivered these punchlines, Modi neither rolled up his sleeves nor raised his voice in anger. His words appeared more credible as a result.

There is a famous Bollywood song, '*Tadbeer se bigdi hui taqdeer bana le*', whose lines can be translated roughly into English as, 'Have no fear, you can rewrite your fate if you have the right strategy.' But then, successful leaders do not just rely on luck and destiny. The beautiful song uses two important Urdu words—taqdeer, or destiny, and tadbeer, which roughly translates to an ingenious device or method to overcome obstacles. Successful leaders like Modi rely more on tadbeer than taqdeer.

There is one unforgettable lesson from this saga that needs to be recounted and repeated. It is not enough for a leader to be courageous and confident on his own, nor is it possible for a lone soldier to win a war. To gain victory, supporters and followers must also be full of courage and confidence. And this cannot be achieved by mere rhetoric. It is important to convince each individual that he has the power to change things. During his rallies across the country, Modi never failed to ask the audience, 'Will you allow this to continue? Will things go on as they are? Will you not reject and punish the self-centred, greedy, family-oriented and dishonest leaders who have cheated, misled and exploited you? Will you not throw them out?' He got a resounding yes on every occasion. These events helped reinforce the confidence of his supporters as well.

Modi never boasted about his strengths or his power. He kept repeating that he is confident of victory because the ordinary Indians who want change are with him. But to be able to motivate people like he did, one needs positive thinking, self-belief and optimism.

It is said that hope does not fade away till the last breath.

But it is equally true that one's breath can rapidly fade away if there is no hope. To achieve victory, it is important to nurture positive thinking and optimism. Modi displayed these skills commendably as he avoided the traps laid by his rivals and refused to respond to many allegations levelled against him; instead, he chose to focus on communicating his message of change and hope. During public rallies in Hajipur and Chhapra in Bihar on 30 April 2014, Modi said: 'These elections are about a new kind of optimism. This is about hope, optimism and change.' A few days later in West Bengal, Modi played around with words and said: '*Badla nahin, badlav*.' That would roughly translate to, 'Change, not revenge.' Modi kept insisting that his only agenda is development. In May 2014 in Domariyaganj, Uttar Pradesh, he asked Hindus and Muslims not to fight with each other but come together to fight poverty. Around this time he also asserted during a rally in Amethi that he had come to sow seeds of hope amongst the youth. And, by constantly using references to half-filled glasses, he convinced the ordinary Indian that he could indeed bring about the change that they were hoping for.

Projecting a credible image was no less significant. Modi continuously spread his image of being a decisive leader through his massive rallies. He worked really hard to build trust and credibility amongst voters. During the famous rally in Hajipur, he said that it was more important to save the nation than to save a government, and this task could be achieved not by a hapless but by a strong government. Modi kept reminding people how governments that failed to deliver on promises could only be termed as weak and helpless. He offered himself as a better and more credible candidate by saying, '*Main vaade nahin, iraade lekar aapke saamne aaya hoon* (I have not come to you with promises but with honest intentions).'

Modi reinforced his credibility by not launching personal attacks on most opponents and talking, instead, about a better future for everyone. He did attack Rahul Gandhi sharply and did not spare Sonia Gandhi either. But he left no doubt in anyone's mind that he was 'taking them on' and criticizing them harshly only because he saw them as symbols of a dynastic despotism that had severely crippled Indian democracy and spawned widespread corruption. Throughout the campaign, he projected a decisive yet humble image. He kept repeating in his rallies that the country needed servants, not rulers. He reminded audiences that they had tried having rulers for sixty years and now it was time to try a servant for sixty months. With statements like these, slogans such as '*Abki baar, Modi sarkar*' resounded even more.

Modi was very careful in his choice of words. During a speech at Unnao on 27 April 2014, he told the audience that he was not the type to make tall promises and sell false dreams. In the same speech, he reassured the people that he would do everything to help them realize their dreams. This made his campaign message connect even more strongly with the aspirations of the people. To motivate dispirited Indians, Modi kept harping on change and development during his entire campaign. He also kept asserting that the elections were not being fought by leaders and parties, but by the 125 billion people of India. The positivity of his message was so strong that gradually even cynics began to believe him.

Modi never ceased to say that the elections were all about hope, trust and confidence. Every time he raised the theme of dreams and expectations, doubts about his ability and intentions started disappearing and even weaker speakers were inspired by the confidence he displayed at all times. Gradually, Indians started associating Modi with both competence and credibility, while his opponents were perceived as unreliable and untrustworthy.

Of course, it was not the rhetoric alone that attracted voters. It was also the track record of Modi as the chief minister of Gujarat.

3

Planning

There is an old saying: The winner takes it all. The Hindi version of it is even more evocative: *Jo jeeta wohi sikandar*. The reference, of course, is to Alexander the Great (known as Sikandar in India) who had conquered more than half the world around 2,500 years ago. In the case of big victories like Alexander's and those of many other legendary generals and leaders, the vanquished are condemned to curse their mistakes and fate while the actions of the victor appear miraculous. But the fact is that it was careful advance planning that enabled victors like Alexander to emerge. Even Napoleon, who said that the secret of victory is courage, was known to have made painstaking preparations before any battle or war. And of course, Napoleon is also famous for saying that the word 'impossible' doesn't exist in his dictionary. Bravery and courage are a must, yes, but they alone cannot take you far without proper planning.

There is no doubt that Narendra Modi displayed a lot of courage and audacity during the election campaign and his mannerisms reflected that he, too, doesn't believe in the word 'impossible'. But at the same time, he put in thought and attention to careful planning not just for the big war but also the smaller battles. A big reason behind this historic victory for Modi was meticulous planning. Whether it is an electoral war or a sports' battlefield, you must be well prepared before you take on your opponents. Carelessness here could prove to be extremely costly.

You can use any jargon to describe this planning and formation of strategy but it won't change the fact that you need a clear road map in your head if you want to be victorious. Only you can make this road map, not others. If you want to build a house, an architect can help you prepare a professional blueprint. But he or she would know your tastes, your budget and actual needs only according to what is conveyed. There is only person who would best know the kind of obstacles you might face in your journey and how you can make the most efficient use of your resources. And that is you.

Getting hold of a map is no guarantee that you will find

a secret treasure. Nor will staring at a map enable you to travel across the world. Sure, the experience of others and the maps made by others can be useful guides. But they will not be enough. The final road map for your victory has to be drawn by you. And you need to plan thoroughly to chart the right kind of map.

Many people call this strategy. It is no surprise that the term is used in both war and in sports, where an effective strategy helps you fight better against your opponent and vanquish him or her. It is all about planning and preparation. A successful strategy is all about gaining victory at the end and that is the only yardstick to measure its efficacy. All military leaders or team captains leave their personal stamp by planning and executing individual strategies to defeat opponents.

Thousands of years ago, the Chinese philosopher Sun Tzu identified and listed many key ingredients of a successful war strategy in his book, *The Art of War*. But you can't just blindly adopt what is written in his book in real life. Even Tzu's sage advice has to be tailored to suit your circumstances and your specific requirements.

The first important step to take while preparing for a battle or war is to have a clear and dispassionate knowledge about your strengths and weaknesses as well as those of your rivals. At the same time, you need to be wary of threats and alert to opportunities that might help you score a decisive victory. In modern jargon, this is known as a SWOT analysis: Strengths, Weaknesses, Threats and Opportunities. A general with a good SWOT analysis is usually a victor.

The election campaign run by Modi is proof that you don't need management degrees to fight the most important battles of your life. It is life and our own experiences that teach us a lot. Of course, some people are born leaders and make this assessment instinctively.

One of the key elements of the strategy prepared by Modi was to maintain a scorching pace of campaign right from day one. The idea was to make his opponents wonder how long and how far would this furious and relentless pace be maintained. Many critics suggested that Modi would find it impossible to sustain this pace and would have to sit back and take a breather at some stage. The implications were clear: if you sit back and relax and take it easy, you have as good as lost the battle, no matter how far ahead you were initially. Modi must have been acutely aware of the famous race between the hare and the tortoise, where the much faster hare streaks far ahead of the tortoise in no time. But later, due to his overconfidence, he sits back to relax. We all know what happened after that. Modi never slackened his pace and never even looked back to see how far behind his opponents were. The opponents who were chasing Modi could not figure out what his basic strategy was: to run a 100-metre sprint or a long marathon. The results are out for all to see!

Nobody can deny that Modi displayed clarity of vision, enormous self-belief and a mixture of courage and audacity during the campaign. But he never was assailed by emotional turmoil or self-doubt like Arjuna in the Mahabharata battlefield. Nor did he ever forget that constant hard work alone is not enough; it has to be combined with a strategy in order to capitalize on his strengths as well as exploit the weaknesses of his opponents.

It is to craft and implement this winning strategy that Modi gathered together a core group. The most important member of this group was Amit Shah. He demonstrated how to revive a flailing party by injecting new life and energy into the BJP in the crucial state of Uttar Pradesh, which has the maximum number of MPs in the Lok Sabha and the Rajya Sabha. This state was the fulcrum around which Modi's core strategy revolved. The decision to make Modi a candidate from Varanasi was an inherent part of the strategy. How could Uttar Pradesh voters resist the temptation to have yet another prime minister from their state?

Modi was well aware of his weaknesses while crafting his electoral strategy. He realized that the BJP was not a serious player in states such as Tamil Nadu, Odisha, West Bengal and the northeastern states. Andhra Pradesh was in a flux because of the Telangana agitation. Expectations from Karnataka were not very high. On the other hand, the party appeared very strong in Gujarat, Madhya Pradesh,

Rajasthan and Chhattisgarh. These points were factored into strategy-making at the ground level. Across the country, it was clear that the Indian voter was fed up with the UPA government at the centre. But Modi knew that a mere anti-incumbency sentiment wouldn't be enough to let him capture the throne in Delhi.

Modi's strategy targeted states that offered unique opportunities to his war plan. Uttar Pradesh was a classic example. The people of the state were already completely disenchanted with the young chief minister, Akhilesh Yadav. Cracks and fissures within the ruling Samajwadi Party (SP) had already begun to appear. Even though the party positioned itself in opposition to the UPA regime, the claim looked hollow since the party chief Mulayam Singh Yadav repeatedly came to the rescue of the UPA government. People living in lawless and anarchic conditions in Uttar Pradesh were becoming convinced that this party of vested interests had nothing to do anymore with the welfare of the common man; its only strategy was to somehow escape from the clutches of corruption cases against it that were being investigated by the Central Bureau of Investigation (CBI).

Things were not very different in the other large party in Uttar Pradesh, the Bahujan Samaj Party (BSP). The manner in which BSP head Mayawati and her party stood on the same side as her bitter rival Mulayam and SP to support and save the UPA government raised serious doubts about her real intentions. Of course, it has often been said about Mayawati that her core vote bank never deserts her, no matter what happens. So many political analysts were of the opinion that the looming losses for the SP would not benefit the BJP, but Mayawati and her party.

Modi had sensed for long that he could reap a rich electoral harvest in the state and this was confirmed by his aide and Uttar Pradesh in-charge Amit Shah. As soon as the campaign started, voters saw Mayawati, Mulayam and the Congress all standing in one corner, roundly abusing Modi and losing no opportunity to label him a communalist and fascist. Modi ignored these attacks and kept sending out a positive message of development and good governance to voters in the state. As the campaign started coming to an end, even Modi critics had started suggesting that Mulayam and Mayawati appeared disconnected from the grass-roots voters and were seemingly evading issues of importance to ordinary citizens. Who can now deny that Modi's strategy was a spectacular success?

Something similar happened in the state of Bihar. For well over a decade, the BJP and the Janata Dal (United) (JD[U]) were allies in the state. Together they had ruled Bihar for more than eight years. So the sudden decision of JD(U) president and Bihar Chief Minister Nitish Kumar to snap his party's alliance with the BJP appeared incongruous, and his criticism of Modi did not find many takers. Every time Kumar lambasted Modi for his communalism or for his dictatorial tendencies and warned people against his brazen and unquenchable lust for power, people assumed that Kumar had a secret desire to himself become the prime minister. Of course, like in Uttar Pradesh, many analysts were of the firm opinion that the other major party in Bihar, the Rashtriya Janata Dal (RJD) headed by Lalu Prasad Yadav, and the Congress, would take advantage of the acrimonious split between the JD(U) and the BJP. But Modi thought differently. He had sensed that the ordinary citizen of Bihar was very upset with the manner in which Nitish Kumar had broken the alliance with the BJP. More importantly, like in Uttar Pradesh, the youth of Bihar was fed up of being a mere pawn in the games of identity politics being played by other parties. Development became a bigger issue than Modi's alleged communalism and authoritarianism.

Though after Uttar Pradesh, West Bengal and Tamil Nadu, apart from Maharashtra, have the maximum number of MPs in Parliament, the BJP presence in these states is like that of other national parties—nominal at best. In West Bengal, the battle lines that matter are drawn between the Trinamool Congress (TMC) and the Communist Party of India (Marxist) (CPI [M]). In Tamil Nadu, the main contenders for power have remained unchanged for decades—the Dravida Munnetra Kazhagam (DMK) and the All India Anna Dravida Munnetra Kazhagam

(AIADMK). Similarly, it was known that for the 2014 elections, the forty-two seats of Andhra Pradesh were divided between K.C. Rao, Chandrababu Naidu and Jagan Mohan Reddy after the Telangana agitation. All parties have suffered splits and splintering down the years, which resulted in unexpected alignments and realignments. It did not make sense to make these states the principal targets for a BJP victory by committing huge resources, time and manpower.

The manner in which the Bharat Vijay (Striving for Victory) rallies were planned reflected these ground realities. They were organized in such a way that the morale of workers and supporters would keep going up and there would emerge a kind of competition between organizers of different venues to host a more powerful or successful show. A number of volunteers and professionals aligned to Modi's cause were entrusted with specific tasks. Meticulous planning was followed by closely supervised implementation. The success of one rally spurred on the organizers of the next venue. The venues also were chosen carefully, keeping history in mind, and Modi always made references to historic events related to the venues and talked about the local issues and problems in great detail. For example, during the rally in Gaya, Bihar, on 27 March 2014, he referred to the fact that it was the 'land of Buddha' that 'gave the message of peace to the world'. And he never failed to address the special concerns, aspirations and worries of the young voters. He also made it a point to don the traditional garb of the states he visited, a practice he continues even after his election as the prime minister.

The reality is that there were many smaller mantras hidden inside this big victory mantra. Successful generals have always distinguished between strategy and tactics and to know when to employ what. Tactics is the art of taking quick, short-term decisions to face sudden threats or to take advantage of newly emerged opportunities. It is easy to change one's tactics at anytime, but strategies are meant to be long term. A good general rarely changes his strategy. Changing strategy halfway through the battle implies that something was basically wrong with the original strategy. Modi understood and implemented this efficiently and ruthlessly.

To make the best possible use of limited time and to always be ready to exploit new opportunities are part of any good strategy. The English poet Rudyard Kipling wrote a famous poem, 'If', that has the following lines:

> If you can fill the unforgiving minute
> With sixty seconds' worth of distance run,
> Yours is the Earth and everything that's in it,
> And—which is more—you'll be a Man, my son!

We don't know if Modi has read the poem but his

actions throughout the election campaign suggested that he understood the importance of these lines. Virtually all twenty-four hours of the day were planned carefully and there was an effort to make use of each minute. There was hardly any free moment available to Modi but whatever little time he squeezed out for eating or rest was used to acquire more information and quell minor revolts and scuffles in the party.

4

Tireless Work and Extreme Self-discipline

The sheer pace at which Narendra Modi led and managed the election campaign over a nine-month period is unprecedented in the history of Indian democracy. In the final forty-five days of his campaign, Modi addressed 196 rallies spread across twenty-five states. Often, after finishing a rally in one state, he would have to address another one in a far-off state involving hectic travel in a short period of time. In the early days of the campaign, his critics pointed out that no one could sustain that kind of pace over a long period and a time would inevitably come when Modi would be exhausted and compelled to take time off. Some even sarcastically said that Modi was making the mistake of running a marathon as if it were a 100-metre sprint. But Modi did it.

Modi was well aware of the risks and dangers he was exposing himself to by maintaining that scorching pace. For one, it was imperative that his physical health stay on course. Maintaining good health during continuous gruelling tours would not have been possible without a healthy diet and setting aside adequate time to recharge his batteries.

It was also probable that some external factors could come up which would disrupt a programme or a rally. It was the express responsibility of his campaign managers to ensure that such disruptions were isolated and not allowed to affect subsequent rallies and tours. Not just the prime ministerial candidate, but even his followers and colleagues could not afford to drop their guard even for one moment during the long campaign process.

Evidently, all this required an extraordinary level of discipline. Whenever confronted with a formidable challenge, people and organizations are said to work on a 'war footing'. That is because it is accepted that trained soldiers practise and maintain the highest levels of discipline. Modi, too, conducted his electoral campaign like a war, with him and his followers maintaining all the discipline that trained soldiers display on the battlefield. Between 15 September 2013 and 10 May 2014, Modi addressed 437 big and small rallies. On any given day, he would address an average of four rallies. He travelled more than 3 lakh kilometres across twenty-five states to be able to do this. If one adds all the other meetings and public events that he attended, the total works out to about 5,827[1]. During this intense and hectic period, Modi spent just ten days in his hometown, Ahmedabad. Even those ten days were used to address 3D hologram rallies that were telecast live across the country.

Modi's planning and extreme discipline was accompanied by smart choices. Since the Bihar chief minister, Nitish Kumar, had launched the fiercest attacks on Modi, the rallies organized in Kumar's state were called 'Hunkar' (challenge) rallies. In Uttar Pradesh, the rallies were named 'Bharat Vijay', the reason being that since Uttar Pradesh sends the most MPs (eighty) to the Parliament, victory (vijay) in the state was the key to victory in India (Bharat). In Maharashtra, the BJP-Shiv Sena alliance challenged old bastions by organizing 'Maha Garjana' (thunderous roar) rallies. In Karnataka, the local term for rally, 'gessi', was used while Andhra Pradesh also saw the use of a Telegu nomenclature, 'geri'. Even in Arunachal Pradesh, which is a site of border dispute between India and China, the term 'Bharat Vijay' was used deliberately to send a strong message

[1]Source: http://timesofindia.indiatimes.com/news/Narendra-Modis-electoral-milestone-437-rallies-3-lakh-km/articleshow/34400255.cms

to China. Using locally evocative terms was designed to attract local citizens and make them connect better with Modi's ultimate goal. The repeated use of the word 'victory' was inspired, as it drilled into voters the message that nothing less than total victory and an absolute majority would do.

It is fashionable to say *'ekla chalo'* (walk alone) when one faces a formidable challenge and has to achieve a goal that appears distant. But successful leaders know different. Victory is not possible by waging lone battles; it is crucial to attract smart and dependable partners and followers who can share one's workload. Be it sports or business or governance, a successful leader knows that building a team with a diverse set of people with different skill sets is important. This aspect of Modi was hardly ever recognized or acknowledged before the elections. He stitched up a powerful team that included paan-chewing and bidi-smoking grass-roots warriors, low-profile bureaucrats, seasoned management professionals, urban entrepreneurs and young and dynamic IT professionals. The manner in which Modi formed and inspired this diverse team to treat the election almost like a Champions' Trophy match that has to be won is simply amazing.

Work on the Modi campaign had started as far back as 2010. Mumbai-based entrepreneur Rajesh Jain and his Bengaluru-based counterpart B.G. Mahesh were convinced by 2010 that Modi was the best candidate to be the next prime minister of India. Jain had become famous in 1999 when he sold his Internet portal IndiaWorld to leading ISP provider Satyam Infoway for ₹499 crore. Mahesh ran a multilingual online portal called Oneindia. Both Jain and Mahesh had advanced degrees from the United States. From 2010, they had started working on their own, as enthusiastic volunteers, on Modi's Mission 272+ plan that eventually came true in 2014. This reflected Modi's strongly held viewpoint that it was important to seek a clear mandate rather than start a campaign dependent on allies. Research by Jain and Mahesh pinpointed about 350 seats where the BJP had a reasonable chance of winning. It was these 350 seats on which Modi concentrated most of his energy.

Critics had for long argued that Modi was incapable of working with others because he was too authoritarian. But if one looks closely and objectively at the 2014 election campaign, it becomes clear that Modi is a master at forming competent teams and making them work. For example, the kind of skills that Amit Shah quietly displayed in Uttar Pradesh to achieve a stupendous, record-breaking electoral win was a classic display of how teamwork and relentless pursuit delivers results. Along with Piyush Goyal and Smriti Irani, Shah ensured that video raths (rallies centred around a specially equipped vehicle) delivering Modi's core message travelled across more than 75 per cent of Uttar Pradesh's villages even before the start of 2014.

Smriti Irani was given the task of launching a multimedia campaign called 'Mere Sapnon Ka Bharat' (India of my Dreams). In this, hundreds of thousands of young Indians made small videos talking about the ideal India of their dreams, which were uploaded and shared online. This campaign led to a strong belief that the Modi campaign was not a centralized effort but a collective campaign by ordinary Indians to realize their aspirations. Piyush Goyal, meanwhile, micro-managed the entire advertisement campaign for Modi, spread across newspapers, television, radio and the Internet. Seasoned bureaucrat K. Kailashnathan kept an eagle eye on the proceedings from behind the scenes. This core team took the help of experienced and successful advertising professionals according to their requirements. Prasoon Joshi, Sam Balsara and Piyush Pandey were some of the top ad professionals closely involved in this exercise.

There is no doubt that the Modi campaign was conducted on a war footing. But it is important to point out one important thing—while discipline is a must, it will not work if it is imposed on others. Discipline has to come from within. To deliver better results, positive thinking, hope and trust in one's mentor matters a lot as well.

Modi motivated hundreds of thousands of ordinary workers to fight as disciplined soldiers by setting a personal example. He was like a general—always in command but never aloof, inspired and inspiring at the same time, brimming with self-confidence and exuding infectious enthusiasm. This was what galvanized his army of foot soldiers and team of lieutenants.

5

Sense of Service and Duty

For centuries, Indians have admired and even revered those who have sacrificed their family lives and other worldly pursuits to dedicate their lives to social and national service. Someone who tirelessly performs his responsibilities without thought of personal reward is always put on a pedestal. It was the manifestly ascetic behaviour of Mahatma Gandhi that endeared him to millions during the freedom struggle. Since he was considered to be above narrow self-interest, nobody questioned his decisions. In his letters, his writings and public speeches, Bapu always emphasized that selfless love towards others and the ability to perform assigned tasks with devotion were the best attributes. A favourite bhajan of the Mahatma goes like this:

Vaishnava jan to tene kahiye je
Peerh paraayi jaane re
Par dukhe upkaar kare toh yeh
Mann abhimaan na aane re

This would roughly translate into English as:

The true devotee of God is one
Who understands the problems and pains of others
And who always helps the needy
Without any pride or sense of entitlement

During the battle in the Mahabharata, when Arjuna was in a dilemma about fighting against his own family and wanted to quit the battlefield, Lord Krishna had motivated him by saying, 'Don't worry about victory or defeat, performing your duty without any expectation of rewards is the most important thing.' In other words, the person who rises above self-interest and faces all challenges with a sense of duty and determination is the one who eventually succeeds.

These traits become even more critical during times of war. The soldier who worries about his family and his worldly assets can never fight fearlessly. It is only the one who selflessly performs his duty who can motivate his partners and followers to have faith and lead them to eventual victory. The martyrs who willingly walked to the gallows during the freedom struggle were well aware that they were fighting for a cause that was much bigger than their individual selves. Someone who is willing to sacrifice his or her life for a larger cause often ends up defeating more powerful enemies. Modi had learnt these lessons of history very well. He made a concerted, determined effort to bring these lessons that had long been forgotten into mainstream discourse.

Anyone talking about service, respect, patriotism and national pride was considered by cynics as being either a naive idealist or a charlatan. When Modi proclaimed at a rally in Pasighat, Arunachal Pradesh, on 22 February 2014, that he was willing to sacrifice his life to protect this land, his critics slammed him as a demagogue who was trying to incite ultra-nationalist sentiments so that ordinary citizens would ignore the real issues and start leaning towards the BJP. But as the campaign gathered momentum, the seemingly obsolete words and slogans started to have a magnetic impact on people. Along with it came another fundamental question that troubled the people of India: was it not true that that selfish and opportunist elitists had conspired to erase ideals and basic values from the national discourse? Hadn't an obsession with worldliness unleashed monumental levels of corruption? Modi presented a sharp contrast to this.

Modi continuously spread his image of being a decisive leader through his massive rallies. He worked really hard to build trust and credibility amongst voters.

His advisers and he understood the importance of constantly communicating positive messages to Indians who were worried about their and their families' future. They knew it was important to sustain their hopes and optimism. This approach was reflected in his physical gestures during public meetings and in his style of oratory that interacted directly with people. He would ask people repeatedly how change could come about and say: 'Would you not break your bonds with people who broke their promises?'

Modi's mannerisms and way of communicating with people was in sharp contrast to that of his opponents. He never spoke along the lines of: 'We have done so much for you, so give us back your votes in return'. Like the former American president, John F. Kennedy, who said, 'Ask not what the country can do for you, ask what you can do for the country', he exhorted people to individually start contributing to the nation and its progress. This was evocative of the manner in which Swami Vivekananda had exhorted Indians more than a century ago to 'Arise, awake and stop not till the goal is reached'.

This ensured that Modi's electoral campaign no longer remained a purely political one but became a call for national awakening. In contrast, the rival Congress tried hard to make use of the 'Bharat Nirman' series of ads for its campaign. But they failed to strike a chord with ordinary citizens and voters, who saw the campaign as a mere advertising gimmick, since the ads didn't even make an effort to connect with basic values, ideals and the spirit of service, hope and trust. Modi's mantra proved enormously successful because he constantly reminded voters of the era gone by when Indians had selflessly sacrificed their all to liberate their country from British rule. And he did this without overusing strong words such as duty, patriotism and sacrifice.

The famous poet Allama Iqbal, in his one of his better-known nazms, 'Bal-e-Jibril', has named 'strong vision' as the number one weapon in the armory of a successful leader:

Nigaah buland,
Sukhan dil nawaaz
Jaan pursouz
Ye hai rakht-e-safar
Mir-e-karawan ke liye

(Strong vision,
Soothing words,
And a passionate, restless soul
Nothing else does the leader of a caravan require
For the journey)

Modi made a continuous effort to encourage the ordinary Indian to become an integral part and member of rebuilding India. The average citizen was persuaded that his personal fortunes will change only when he contributes to changing the fortunes of the country. The voter was made to realize that the best way to improve one's personal lot and that of one's community was to work for the country. Modi's critics kept portraying him as a divisive and communal figure, apart from being an authoritarian fascist. But these charges failed to make an impression on voters because by starting a more positive debate, Modi had made these issues redundant.

Modi never lost an opportunity to keep hammering positive messages, even at cynical voters who were not swayed by the Modi campaign. Although rivals kept saying that it was impossible for Modi and the BJP to win a majority and asked people not to waste their votes on him, Modi had an effective reply to silence his critics and opponents. For example, during the Hajipur rally in Bihar, Modi confidently asserted that the elections were not merely about numbers and arithmetic, but also the chemistry of 125 billion Indians. The results proved him right.

At almost every public rally, Modi kept asserting that the elections were all about hope, faith and trust. Every time he used his oratorical skills to invoke these sentiments, even cynics were compelled to shed their negative thoughts. Each time the word 'trust' was associated with Modi, his opponents began to be viewed as essentially untrustworthy.

It must be understood here that it was not just a play of words and oratorical skills that captured the hearts and minds of voters. Modi's visible track record as chief minister of Gujarat persuaded most Indians that the man was above narrow family attachments and vested interests and could be trusted. There never was any need to find proof for his words when, on 10 April 2014, Modi declared at a rally in Arrah, Bihar, 'I was born in a poor family so I understand the pain and indignity of poverty.'

6

Power of New Technology

When one is set to achieve big goals, the smart use of new tools and techniques helps one emerge victorious. In contemporary times, a person who stays constantly in touch with rapid technological changes and uses the latest tools to further his ambitions becomes successful. And in this, Modi has been unquestionably better and smarter than his opponents. From his second tenure as the chief minister of Gujarat onwards, Modi had started extensively using the power of computers and information technology to reduce corruption and increase transparency in governance. Even the recruitment of school teachers was done through a transparent online process. This kind of open governance enthused not just the youth but also sincere government employees. And this experience was utilized to its fullest during the 2014 campaign.

Each time Modi talked about using technology to improve the lives of ordinary people, his voters didn't take it as some esoteric magic. During a speech at the NASSCOM India Leadership Forum delivered on 14 February 2014, Modi said, 'I see the role of IT as a change agent. It empowers. It connects. IT can bind isolated parts of a country; IT can create harmony in society; IT can join people with governments; IT can reduce the gap between demand and supply; IT can bring us closer to precious knowledge.'

For people used to mobile phones and the Internet, Modi's words had a strong touch of credibility. The ease with he talked about the practical uses of technology enabled him to connect better with young and urban Indians. Whenever he explained how technology could solve real-life problems, people would immediately relate to the examples given by him. For instance, when, during the closing ceremony of the Golden Jubilee celebrations of the Bar Council of India on 1 March 2014, he said, 'Convergence of technology and the judicial system is the need-of-the-hour.' He laid emphasis on the need to go digital and adopt online analysis of legal cases. He added that a dissemination of legal knowledge to the common man would go a long way in improving the law and order situation in the country.

While his opponents were busy trying to demonize him, Modi kept talking about how he welcomed technology and was constantly fascinated by it, and how he kept trying new innovations. This was like a breath of fresh air for Indians, particularly the youth, as Modi was talking a language they understood well. On 26 February 2014, while launching an 'e-nagar project' in Gandhinagar, he said, 'This century is going to be linked with the virtual world. Maybe in the days to come you will have virtual malls and digital manufacturing. Change is coming fast and we need our urban areas to keep pace with these changes.'

A generation used to buying books, music and clothes from Amazon and Flipkart, who purchase train and movie tickets online, could instantly relate to Modi.

The manner in which Modi successfully harnessed the power of technology and new media is a classic example of the potential of social media if properly harnessed and integrated in strategy. Modi had realized that the mainstream (particularly) English media and TV channels were opposed to him. They were busy demonizing him through constant debates on communalism versus secularism and democracy versus fascism. Modi knew he had to look at other modes of media to be able to communicate his message to voters.

It is obvious that Modi had kept an eagle eye on how new technology and social media was being used across the world. Whether it was the Arab Spring or the election-related protests in Iran or the demonstrations in Ukraine and Russia, Facebook and Twitter had demonstrated how one could break the shackles imposed by mainstream media.

Modi adopted a two-pronged strategy during his campaign. The first was the widespread use of public rallies and meetings. This was to be done across nine months in a kind of blitzkrieg of rallies. Wherever he couldn't physically be present, Twitter, Facebook and other tools of social media were used efficiently to spread his message. Social media had earlier been successfully used during the Jan Lokpal agitation led by Anna Hazare and Arvind Kejriwal. Modi was never embarrassed at adopting the SMS strategy used by the Anna team and, in fact, he improved their techniques to greater effect.

To be able to succeed in the medium of technology, one must have the ability or skill to make an impact using as few words as possible. People who are surfing and riding the waves of the information highways do not have the time to wait. All one has is 140 characters to either praise or damn someone on Twitter. This limit doesn't leave any scope for long-drawn debates or question-answer sessions. But that doesn't mean that Twitter cannot be used to inflict deep wounds and as a Brahmastra to cripple opponents. Virtually every statement by a leader and the buzz around it can be used by the so-called tweeple to reach millions of people. This game continues on other social media platforms such as blogs and Facebook, which allow for a greater number of words to be employed.

The irony was that even as his opponents kept attacking him, calling him dictatorial and fascist, Modi successfully used social media to project himself as democratic. During a meeting organized by FICCI on 15 January 2014, Modi publicly exhorted all participants to use Facebook and Twitter to send him suggestions so that he could integrate their ideas with his own agenda. Enthusiastic followers were prompt in replying to these messages and suggestions that ordinary Indians genuinely felt they were truly connected with a leader like Modi.

Modi didn't spare any social media tools. Be it Google Hangouts or 3D hologram rallies, Modi used all opportunities to reach out to people he couldn't interact with directly in public meetings. The venues for the virtual rallies were nothing less than glamorous Bollywood-like sets. Standing atop a lavishly mounted podium, Modi's hologram would address the virtual rallies in his inimitable style as if he was actually present. The latest technology was used to record these speeches and broadband, DTH and video conferencing were utilized to stream them to give viewers an uninterrupted experience. About 100 destinations were chosen for each of these high-tech rallies and outfitted with podiums that had 40x35 feet screens. The software used for all this was such that one didn't need 3D glasses to watch it.

People standing near the screens used to feel as if Modi was standing right there and talking to them. It is estimated that Modi used about 100 of these rallies to reach out to more than 10 million people. Besides, hundreds of thousands of people watched the rallies on their laptops and smartphones. No one had used this kind of technology so extensively for an election campaign in India before this. Modi's critics kept saying that he was merely imitating American campaign styles and was wasting money on needless gimmicks. But his fabulous victory proved his critics completely wrong.

Supporters of Modi also organized the famous 'Chai pe Charcha' meetings, where the Modi visage was much larger than the images seen in the 3D rallies. When such huge screens were erected in many carefully selected locations, was it any surprise that people became curious about what exactly was going on? This 'new' kind of theatre became quite popular with the masses. Quite simply, targeting a location where about 1,500-odd people could gather ensured that a collective audience of lakhs of potential voters was present for the events. Modi used these rallies to communicate serious issues with the people.

The first 3D rally that Modi used in April 2014 to present himself as a serious candidate was revealing in the way he used social media to display his inimitable style. People were compelled to sit up and take notice when he announced, 'Please do not vote for me on the basis of caste, clan, creed or religion.' Critics who habitually branded him as a communal and fascist politician who used divisiveness to win votes were stumped for answers when Modi said this. This virtual rally was 'telecast' live in more than 100 locations and played a big role in countering negative propaganda about him. When people saw Modi himself appealing to people not to vote for him on the basis of caste and religion, they were compelled to ask, 'What is he asking us to vote for?' The answer, repeatedly proclaimed by Modi, was: development.

Some days later, Modi dedicated a virtual rally at Lakhimpur Kheri and Shahjahanpur in Uttar Pradesh on 14 April 2014 to the memory of the great Dr Bhimrao Ambedkar. Though he never asked for votes directly in the name of identity politics, Modi was acutely aware that the caste issue was a sensitive one and people who were earlier oppressed should never feel neglected or insulted by anything he said. Whenever he talked about development for everybody, Modi constantly underlined that the upliftment of the oppressed classes was linked to economic progress for all sections. Modi used this rally to reassure Dalits that his call to go beyond caste politics didn't mean that he was neglecting their concerns. Rather, he sent out a strong message that vested interests and opportunist politicians actually insulted the legacy of legendary leaders such as Dr Ambedkar who had fought for the oppressed classes. One week later, Modi used a 3D rally to suggest that the country badly needed a more mature level of politics. His message was unstated but clear: people in power were behaving like irresponsible and immature puppets.

By the time the fourth rally was organized, people had become quite curious about the content, format and message of this twenty-first century innovation. Though Modi always stuck to his core message in every rally, he also used each occasion to say something new and interesting. The Ghalib-like quality of Modi's oratory connected with ordinary Indians ensured that a large number of people were attracted to his 3D rallies. Before the end of April, the fifth 3D rally was over and Modi had started exhorting people: 'Go out and break all records of voting.'

Sensing the pulse of the youth, the responsibility for the lyrics of the campaign song for Modi were given to lyricist and screenwriter Prasoon Joshi, who has been associated with hit movies such as *Rang De Basanti*. To add punch, this video actually used Modi's voice and his face at strategic moments. For viewers, it looked less like an ad and more like an informal conversation with Modi, where his vision and his promises were presented in an entertaining manner. Instead of seeking votes in the name of the party or the leader, people were asked to think about patriotism and national dignity while making their choices. It is no surprise that the words '*Main desh nahin mitne doonga; main sheesh nahin jhookne doonga*', from the BJP election anthem became immensely popular. Who could dare raise a voice against this kind of patriotism?

Close to fifteen crore young Indians participated in the 2014 elections. Out of this, at least ten crore were familiar with new social media. It has been estimated that about 75 per cent of these voters opted for Modi in urban and semi-urban areas. Modi was successful because he understood the power of the winds of change.

7

Power of Dreams

There is a particularly poignant line penned by one of Punjab's finest poets, Avtar Singh Sandhu 'Pash', '*Sab ton khatarnak hunda hai sad supniyon da mar jana* (Nothing is more dangerous than the death of our dreams).' Indeed, life isn't worth living without dreams—neither for an individual nor for a community. All of us begin dreaming in childhood and keep weaving dreams through adulthood and old age. There are some dreams that are strictly personal and some concern those who share our lives or whose lives intersect ours. These are dreams of prosperity and happiness. We chart our course to different destinations dreaming along the way and the desire to fulfil these dreams is what sustains us through trials and tribulations. The Bible has an evocative line: 'Your old men will dream dreams; your young men will see visions' (Joel 2:28). This makes clear that it is essential to have foresight and farsightedness to realize one's dreams. This is what vision means. Only after imagining what the future is likely to be can we hope to prepare adequately for the emerging challenges. This was the role played by ancient Indian seers, aptly called rishis, meaning 'those who can see'. Today we have almost forgotten that it was implicit that they could see what others—younger or inexperienced—couldn't. Theirs was to show others the path.

Nothing can be accomplished in social or political life without dreams and vision, without farsightedness. This is the most important quality required of a leader. All the great leaders in the history of mankind are recognized as visionaries. When a dream is shared with many by a charismatic leader, it becomes a vision. For the common man vision means a shared dream about the future. It is these dreams that empower us to unite and cope with difficulties. Memories of shared struggles and of dangerous battles fought to achieve common goals keep alive shared dreams.

Martin Luther King Jr, who waged a heroic and successful war against racial discrimination in the US, had revitalized the hopeless African-Americans just by proclaiming, 'I have a dream!' His was a dream of equality and social justice. Years later a young Indian prime minister, Rajiv Gandhi, borrowed his words to galvanize his audiences, 'I too have a dream!' This was a dream of prosperous India, an India free from corruption, an India technologically advanced, well prepared to enter the twenty-first century brimming with self-confidence.

Many great leaders have dreamt similar dreams before this, dreams of national progress and improving lives. Mahatma Gandhi had the dream to 'wipe each tear from every eye'. He dreamt of self-reliant villages, prosperous farmers and craftsmen, and of reaching out to the man standing at the end of a long line of oppressed and dispossessed. Guaranteeing work to each pair of hands and fair wages to those who toiled was also part of this dream.

Gandhi declared Jawaharlal Nehru to be his political heir, knowing fully that Nehru had dreams of his own, very different from Gandhi's dreams. Nehru dreamt of large dams, factories and modern cities. He was fond of calling these the new temples, mosques and churches of new India. He thought this was the only hope to liberate Indians from the shackles of age-old servitude. Nehru's dreams filled people with hope and the Five Year Plans invigorated them in the aftermath of Independence.

It is important for us to understand that there was no essential conflict between these two sets of dreams—they were in fact complementary. Unfortunately, after the martyrdom of Gandhi, no one came forward to accept the ownership of his dream. Nehru's dreams of modernity pushed Gandhi's vision beyond the margins. Nehru ruled for almost two decades and after a short gap was followed by his daughter Indira Gandhi. Not many had time to worry about the Gandhian dream.

Sardar Vallabhbhai Patel had the dream to rid India of the vestiges of feudal rule and to forge a strong, united India integrating in the union over 550 princely states. He also dreamt of providing good governance in independent India. He strove to adapt the steel frame of bureaucracy erected by the colonial masters to the changed needs of the new India—a democratic republic. Patel's dream too faded away after his death.

The same fate befell Lal Bahadur Shastri's dreams. He was the prime minister of India for a very short while, but did manage to leave an indelible imprint. Common people still cherish his memory. Shastri dreamt of abolishing hunger and building an India capable of defending its borders. He coined the slogan '*Jai jawan! Jai kisan!*' putting the soldier and the farmer on an equal pedestal. India was smarting after the humiliating defeat at the hands of the Chinese in the border war of 1962. Shastri succeeded in restoring our lost self-respect after a clash of arms with Pakistan in 1965 in which India emerged victorious. The Tashkent Agreement reflected India's strength, not any weakness. In brief, Shastri's dream was essentially patriotic.

Indira Gandhi had shown the dream of abolishing poverty, melodramatically exhorting Indians, '*Garibi hatao*!' It drew millions to her in the beginning but it didn't take long for the dream to shatter and disillusionment to set in. Slowly the reality dawned on the voters that this was no more than election rhetoric. After the declaration of Emergency, Mrs Gandhi could never recreate the magic of any dream. Even then, it can't be denied that she realized the imperative of preserving the national pride of India and safeguarding its unity and integrity. Be it the Green Revolution or the nuclear test at Pokharan, these were steps undertaken towards the realization of the cherished dream of making India great. The list of Indira Gandhi's flaws and mistakes is indeed very long but this doesn't detract from the fact that she was always prepared to inspire and encourage her fellow citizens in their endeavours. A short while before her tragic assassination, she had declared that she would protect this country with the last drop of blood in her body. No one then had smelt ultra-nationalism or blind chauvinism in the statement. The truth is that the dreams of our prosperity and development are inextricably entwined with patriotism.

Indira Gandhi's son Rajiv Gandhi's dream too remained a mirage. Before he could even make an earnest beginning to realize it, his government was engulfed in myriad controversies. But here it must be conceded that Rajiv, when he debuted, could draw young Indians like a strong magnet because he too had emphasized technological progress and the pride of India equally. The slogan he raised to galvanize the youth was, '*Mera Bharat mahaan*'. Under him, the people of India happily prepared to accept hardships and readied themselves for nation building.

Rajiv's successor, V.P. Singh, had a dream to empower the backward sections of society and to give them their long-denied rights. That was why he decided to implement the recommendations of the Mandal Commission to reserve a certain section of university seats and jobs for the oppressed classes. Unfortunately, he failed to share his dream with the nation and the path he followed dictatorially to realize this dream pushed the country to the brink. The nation was engulfed by riots. Besides, many felt that Singh had been constrained to unleash this Mandal weapon to counter the lethal power of Kamandal—the popular moniker for the Ram Janmbhoomi Andolan sponsored by the BJP. Singh, it seemed, had played what he believed to be a trump card also to neutralize the mass appeal of the Jat leader Devi Lal. The long and short of it is that after this fiasco, the coalition Janata government that was formed could barely complete a full term in office and had no time for dreams.

The next Congress prime minister, Narasimha Rao, dreamt of ridding India of red tape and freeing it from the license permit raj. He wished to accelerate the pace of economic progress by ushering in economic reforms. Regrettably, much before he could complete his term in office, Rao was entangled in several unsavoury scams and scandals. Manmohan Singh, as his loyal finance minister, did make a beginning in liberalizing the economy but the challenge remained.

Narendra Modi understands very well the power of dreams. That is the reason he used a powerful dream as a bedrock for his electoral campaign. Truth be told, this dream is the distilled essence of many a past and present aspiration. It refracts the visions unveiled by Swami Vivekananda and Sri Aurobindo and is charged with the restless energy of youth that fired revolutionaries Bhagat Singh, Ramprasad Bismil and Ashfaqulla. This dream encompasses hundreds of aspirations and ambitions and countless hopes. It has no place for the conflict between cities and villages, nor is industry and agriculture arrayed against one another in dubious battle. This dream reminds us of what remains to be done—unfinished tasks that we can ill afford to postpone. This is a dream of unity and development, of a resurgent and great India, of the welfare of the people and of good governance.

The occasion chosen for this task was very appropriate. Sardar Vallabhbhai Patel is remembered till today for his heroic contribution in safeguarding the unity and integrity of India. On 24 March 2014, while laying down the foundation of a gigantic statue of the Iron Man of India, as Sardar Patel is known, Modi presented the outlines of the India of his dreams. This was a dream none could hesitate in sharing. This was a dream of bringing about unity, grandeur and international prestige.

Throughout his campaign, Modi kept emphasizing that our unity is our greatest strength and the greatest guarantee for a golden future. There is no conflict between this unity and our diversity. He also reminded his audiences across the length and breadth of the land that no tree, however tall, can stand for long if it is cut off from its roots. It becomes weak and can't survive. We, too, can't progress if we disown our cultural heritage. The dream of a nation marching loose confidently on the path of progress is entwined with the dream of inclusive growth.

Sharing his dreams with millions of his compatriots played a very big role in Modi's victory. During his campaign he often paraphrased Rabindranath Tagore, 'Unless we dare to dream, how can we resolve to make them come true?' Our destinations depend on our dreams, our dreams help us prepare for the journey with determination, and we persevere tirelessly without flinching to realize them. Dreams help us sustain the morale and to break the shackles of narrow self-interest. They keep alive the impulse to fulfil our patriotic duty. Dreams are an integral part of the winning formula.